Preface

20 years ago, Sarit and I first truly bonded over our appreciation for words. As children, we were obviously writing simplistic poems that rhymed. But the seeds of finding our voices as paper meets pen were sown early. Over the years, he has ushered me into appreciating nuances of Sufi Poetry, while I believe I was the one who encouraged him to finally start a blog.

Words are also the reason our tumultuous courtship found closure in marriage. Because what we could not admit in person, was often easier to convey in prose and poetry. Our homes across the world have been strewn with little notes of affection and apologies that were never verbalized. But this curation of poems is more than the sum of our relationship.

This book exists as a record-keeping device of our separate and collective memories as we take a breath in our on-going journey as individuals and partners.

Our words are now yours.

Table of Contents

Poems

Are You Here

Is that your fragrance in the air?
The tip toeing of heels
in the corridor,
is that you?

Are you cooking a feast?
The scent of curry leaves
wafting from the kitchen,
is that you?

Are you saying a quiet prayer?
Those distant chants,
coming from the other room,
is that you?

Are you beside the Champa flowers?
The freshness of an evening breeze,
blowing from the balcony,
is that you?

The creaking of the chair,
the folds on my bed sheet,
the woman I woke up next to,
is that you?

Maybe it's just me -
imagining things,
dreaming dreams
that we once lived.

By Sarit

Still Here

Scanning the menu for the eleventh time,
I mentally chant the coffee order I will place once you arrive.

I didn't care for our usual table, or the one at which our parents had met.
Picking this cafe was not to evoke memories; just a matter of technicality.
Our separate worlds collide somewhat in central Delhi.

It is a rare evening when the breeze
is pleasant enough to temper the heat.
You arrive dressed casually, precariously resting
your sunglasses (new I assume) at the table.
Place your coffee order - always one of the specials.

I scan your hand for the Tissot I saved up for.
You have it on, but I know, it means nothing anymore.
Just like the small talk that ensues, as we settle
into a new unfamiliar formality in each other's company.

We banter, exchange news about friends
our share neatly divided after the split.
You speak in detail of work trip to Singapore,
I keep quiet about mine to Ladakh.
You look away a lot, distracted,
by the order at the next table, tracing the movement of servers under the shaded trellis.
I sense the absence of warmth from your words,
even though you have not uttered one unfriendly note.
But this stings sharper, wounds more than insults.

You have already time-traveled to a world where we are friends,
as if nothing came before (nothing will come after).
But I am still here, living in that after.
On some nights, my body needs to be prompted to breathe.
Recycled hope keeps me afloat, and denial has not yet made way for grief.

It still doesn't feel permanent, like death.
Even though you have told me through actions and words that it must be.
Even when I have shared parts of me with others,
that I thought could only be shared with you.
And if truth be told, I don't even know if I can bear
to re-acquaint the new me with this new you.

But today is not that conversation.
Just a catch-up, before you leave the city again.
So I play my part, and we keep it on the surface,
I offer you a ride to the nearest metro but you are in the mood to walk.
I sit in the car just a moment too long,
watching you walk away, into a future, without me.

By Neetika

Jag se Juda

Ek pagli bawari si ladki
Jag se juda sawari si ladki
Takti nazro se beparwah ladki
Lamha lamha jhagadti ladhki
Bikharti zulfo ko sawarti ladki
Pal pal jeet ti,pal pal haarti ladki

Kabhi behen, kabhi beti, kabhi ardhagini banti ladki
Har din thodi aur aurat si dikhti ladki
Har pehar naye spane sajati ladki
Har shamm apekshao ki aagosh mai samati ladki
Tute sapne samet ti,khud bikharti ladki
Behad pareshaan fir bhi muskurati ladki

Mujhse baat karti, mujhe pukarti ladki
Mujhe yaad karti, mujhe bhulati ladki
Mere aakhri aadhar si mere zindagi ke saar si
Mere pehle pyaar si
Ek pagli bawari si ladki
Jag se juda sawari si ladki

By Sarit

Tum

Agar subah ki sondhi dhoop
Cotton ke parde se jhagadte
Kamre mai aa jati tumharein
Toh kya kehti tumse?
Yehi ki mujhse door mat jaya karo

Agar mere kandhe ki jagah rakha takiya
Lihaf ke bheetar se jhakte
Kano mai gunguna pata tumharein
Toh kya kehta?
Yehi ke mai intezaar kar raha hun tumhara

Agar din ki pehli chai ki pyali,
Tumharein hothon ko chune se pehle
Kuch keh pati tumse
Toh kya kehti?
Yehi ke tum bin subah aati toh hai, par roshan nahi hoti

Agar karorho ki bheed ke beech,
Achanak takra jata tumse
Meri aankhen tumhari aankho ko kahani sunati
Aur yeh kehti,
Tum ek adhoorein mujh ka,ek pura saar ho

By Sarit

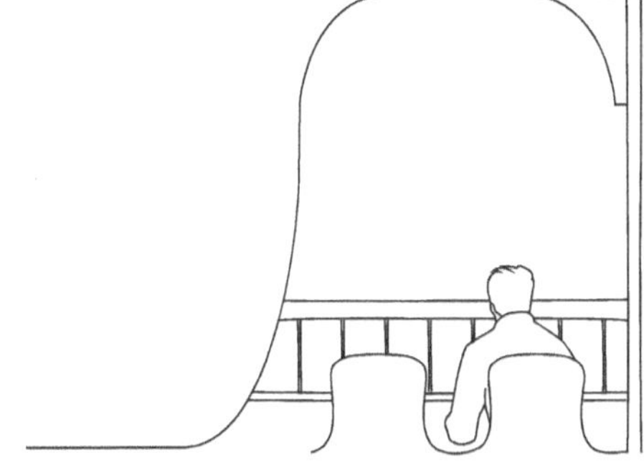

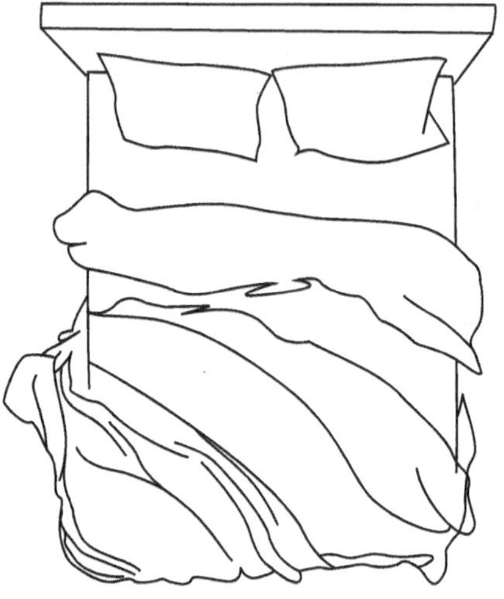

Fursat Ka Sawan

Saawan ki subah
Bikhre bistar par bikhri hui si tum
Bikhra sa mai, bikhre se hum

Chaadar mai sar chupa gum ho jati tum,
Chaadar tale tumko dhoondta, gum hota mai,

Dheeme dheeme khudko samet ti karwat leti tum
Berang pani mai chai ki patiyon ka bhura rang bhapta mai

Adrak ki chai ki khushbu se uthti tum
Chai ke khali pyale ko dekh muskurata mai

Balcony mai khade barish ki bunde ginti tum
Khdiki ke pare, barish mai gungunate tumhai sunta mai

Badlo tale kalpanao ki udhan bharti tum
Zameen par khade tumko gagan choomte takta mai

Woh bikhra bistar, woh silwato wali chadar
Woh chai ka pyala, woh bundo se bhigi balcony
Woh tum, woh mai, woh sawan ki subah

By Sarit

I hope you smile

At times I wonder if long after I am gone,
when you and a friend meet at the Little Branch Cafe,
and if she mentions me, in between a sip
of latte and a bite of a croissant -
what would you tell her about me?

What would you say about
the kind of man I was.
Did you think I was a good husband?
Did you think I was a good father?
What stories would you remember me by?

I wish you would tell her about my love for flowers,
and that time in San Fran when I picked a deep
indigo rose for you - a flower that has since dried
out over the years, sandwiched between chapters of

Padma Laxmi's love life and what we ate. You could
tell her about our pizza quests, and the fact that we
had our best one in a rustic old basement in Slovenia -
a trip that became the reason I finally got a driving license.

Don't forget to mention the baking, and the intoxicating
cocktails through the pandemic, and for years after.
But maybe just maybe you'll tell her about the night
you were upset about the dinner at my parents. We left

mid-meal, quarreling all through our one hour ride back home
When we did reach home, I left, switched off my phone,
drove away into the night not knowing if I would return.
All I knew was I wanted as much distance between us

as possible. When I did return hours after I don't know
why I thought it was ok. I ran from confronting your pain,
comforting you when you were in pain. That you would have
found a way without me. I was too cowardly to find it with you.

Maybe you'll tell her how often I left you, in a sea of tears.
You took days to recover, sometimes months
Maybe you will ponder about a story we did not
get to live. That afternoon you came back home
to find this poem under a stack of books in your study.

I hope that flipping through the pages of your life,
you relive our stories. And I hope they make you smile.

By Sarit

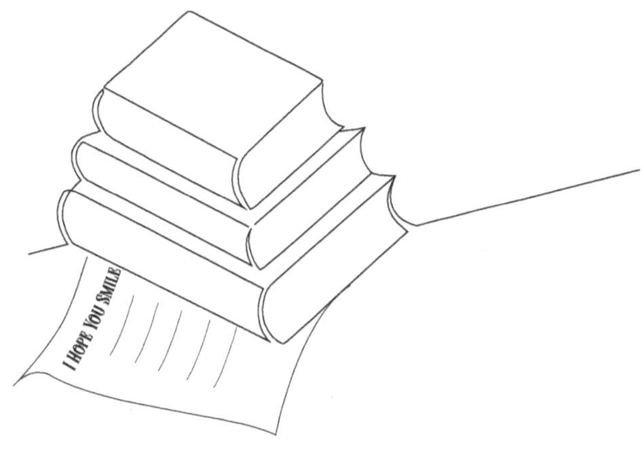

Chajja

Ek Champa ka pedh hai,
ek rassi se buni khaat beechi hai.
Aur bamboo ke dhaache ke sahaaren,
dheeme dheeme badhti ek bel lagi hai.

In pedh podho ka humne
ek parda sa bana rakha hai.
Apni chai ki tapri ko
duniya se chupa rakha hai.

Aksar ek bulbul chajje ke kone se
mujhe takti rehti hai. Jaise hi subah
ki chai khatam hoti hai, udari maar
champa ke pato mai gum ho jati hai.

Maloom hota hai,
ghosla bana liya hai usne.
Kuch chi chi karte bache diye hai.
Ghar basa liya hai usne.

Ab chai ki pyali kamre
mai hi pi jaati hai. Bulbul bhi bekhauf
Champa mai cheepe ghosle
mai daana daalne aati hai.

Kambakht bulbul ne chajja,
Champa, tapri, sab hathiya liya hai.
Bina lease ke kirayedaar ne,
mahine se kiraya bhi nahi diya hai.

Mera bas chale toh nikaal phenku bulbul ko.
Par honsla nahi juta pata. Beeta kal yaad aa jaata hai.
Woh makaan malik yaad aa jaata hai, jisne kabhi
chand rupo ke liye mujhse mera ghar cheen liya tha.

Woh ghar, yaadein jodh kar banaya tha jise.
Woh ghar, kuch haseen lamho se sajaya tha jise.
Woh ghar, jise jab jab bhoolna chaha,
tab tab woh yaad aaya hai mujhe

By Sarit

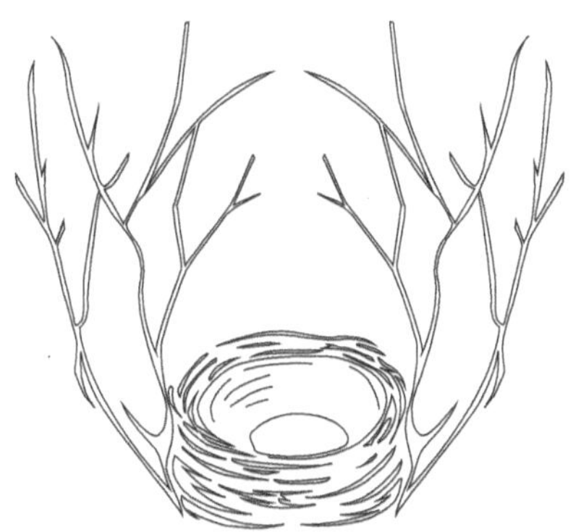

Seasons

It's been a lifetime since I saw you.
Since you left our home to build
a life in the windy city.

A dream you once sacrificed for love.
A dream you lived every day of your life.
A dream that would become a need.

Every day since we got married,
every time Delhi winter hit, every time
dark smog clouds engulfed the balcony,
you'd want to run away. To clear skies,
and a splash of sunshine.

It's been a lifetime of spring, summer,
autumn and winter. Remind me,
which winter did we part ways?

It was winter for sure -
I remember, because my hands froze as I
dragged a suitcase heavy with the weight of responsibility,
down the pavement and across the street.

I remember because all I could think of was the walk back.
All I could think of was how long before the walk back.

Would my suitcase be heavier or lighter?
Would I have packed for days or forever?
Would it still be winter?
Or would the summer sun shine on a beautiful tomorrow?

A tomorrow that comes before we are too old to be young again.
A tomorrow that knows, I want to be a father, even if
I am too scared to say it out loud.

A tomorrow that's ours, through every
spring, summer, autumn and winter.

By Sarit

Faux Pax of Memory

'Where is home for you?' -
Small talk from the anesthesiologist,
encouraging me back into consciousness,
on the dentist's chair.

Inebriated, with a gauze-stuffed mouth,
I describe the condo building,
by Grant Park and Lake Michigan -
a view so rare.

I speak (or perhaps think?) with affection
of the deep dish, the Zoo, the museums, Lincoln Park,
the secret beach by my house, the Chicago Bears.

I have more to say -
about the troubles on the Red line,
spots to view the transient Cherry Blossoms,
the brutal wind, the inconvenience of layers.

When the fog in my brain settles,
recovering on the couch at home,
I realize the faux pax of my memory.

I recognize this manipulation,
of love and longing. These tricks
of the brain are familiar to me.

An indelible connection with
something lost to the past.
I have been in this place previously.

So when I am asked of home at the dentist's office,
in my delirium, I Neetika Wahi, born and raised in India,
living in Toronto, laboriously declare "'Zhicaaacago"

By Neetika

Dichotomy

I know how it goes -
the 'regular' life.

I stay in the center,
delicately in the center,
on the outside.

My insides churn violently,
out of whack from the silence,
I carefully maintain on the outside.

I bow down as they speak of God,
And also nod my head as the atheists protest.

I speak of the sanctity of values
and the need for morals,
then betray both to suit my will.

I harbor desires for authentic friendships,
yet utter innumerable lies to keep them alive.

I know how it goes -
the 'regular' life,
where I muffle tiny truths in my head each day,
and repeat verbatim myths fed by others.

Where I dream of unconditional love,
but keep score of words and wounds.

Where all I truly need is peace within,
yet wander the world seeking it.

By Neetika

Dayraa

Zindagi ke na jaane kitne pal, sisakte hue guzaar diye,
Udne ki khwahish dil mai rakhi thi humesha,
Na jaane kitne lamhe, pedal chalte guzaar diye,

Aaj bhi Kuch andar band sa hai, ked sa,
Na jaane kab riha hoga,
Rihayi ki umeed mai ked yeh haseen pal, yuhi guzaar diye,
Zindagi ke na jaane kitne pal sisakte hue guzaar diye,

Khushi aur gam dono ek se dikhte hai,
Aksar farak samajh nahi aata,
Kai saal Khushiyon ki bheed mai, gamo ko chunte guzaar diye
Zindagi ke na jaane kitne pal sisakte hue guzaar diye,

Mera hona mujhe jhoot lagta hai,
Toote sheshe ke tukdo mai
Har din ek naya Sarit dikhta hai,
Apne aap se apni pehchaan karate, ghanto guzaar diye,
Zindagi ke na jaane kitne pal sisakte hue guzaar diye,

Joh poori ho woh zindagi hoti hai,
Kuch mahine, kuch saal mai toh sirf adhoori hoti hai,
Thoda aur jee ke dekhte hai,
Kuch nayi kahaniya likh ke dekhte hai,
Mujh mein mai aur meri zindagi dono baki hai,
Shayad sheeshe mein dikhti parchayi kuch aur ho,
Yeh banti bigadti zindagi kuch aur ho

By Sarit

Mere Alfaz

Meri likhi pankhtiya kuch badli badli nazar aati hai.
Alfaz to wohi hai, par ek naya matlab samjhati hai.
Kyon meri soch udte udte thak jaati hai,
Kyon aksar khwab dekhte dekhte meri neend toot jaati hai.

Yeh neela aasman, aur aasman mai aag ke gole sa yeh suraj.
Aksar upar betha mujhe ghurta sa rehta hai.
Mann ne kayi baar uksaya ki kood kar nigal ja kambakht ko,
Par jab bhi koshish kari ek badri si cha jaati hai.

Meri ek saheli hai zindagi naam hai,
Aksar mere ghar khelne aati hai,
Jab bhi mai us se jeetne lagta hun,
Na jaane kyon rooth jaati hai,

Kuch ajeeb se sawalo ne gher sa rakha hai,
Yeh poochti hai mujhse ki mai kyon umeed se hun,
Kyon mai zindagi ko rasta dikhata hun,
Zindagi to chanchal hai kisi bhi modh moodh jaati hai,
Meri likhi panktiyan kuch badli badli nazar aati hai

By Sarit

Finding Sarit

I have never felt more stagnant,
than before a big move.
The question what next,
often returns an answer - nothing.

If only I had a crystal ball to
carry me from one what next
to the other. Neither the question
would arise, nor inertia.

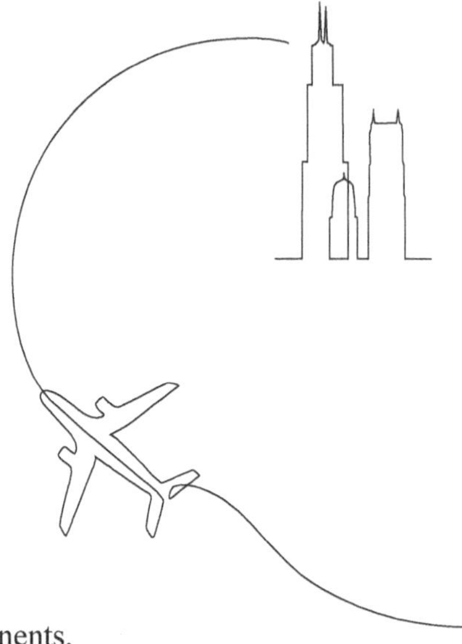

Inertia that rests comfortably
at the cusp of movement and
the lack of it. So comfortably,
the two co-exist.

The most stationary I have stayed,
has been on a 16-hour flight that
took me the furthest I have been.

Out of my home, across seas and continents,
to unfamiliar streets, parks and meadows
that are longing to become my neighborhood.

A neighborhood where the café next door
doesn't know my staple order anymore.
The chef is no longer an acquaintance,
and the bartender doesn't chat me up about
the new boutique gin in town.

My negronis are off balance,
my mojitos too tart,
and the new cocktail menu
just screams of change.

I move from café to café, bar to bar,
until I arrive at that one watering hole
where the mouthfeel of a milk punch,
reminds me of life back home.

Of memories and ties and strings
that I worked so hard to knot
and attach, to my fingers and
limbs and my neck like a noose.

Deep beneath the spirit of moving on,
the feeling of not having moved at all.
Still living in the past and
hoping for a future that is familiar.

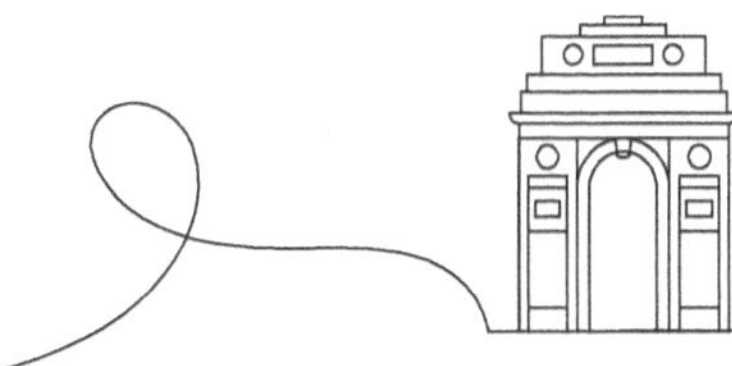

Am I moving backwards?
Am I moving at all?

Does it even matter?
As long as I keep moving
On a journey of finding myself
Losing myself, discovering
and rediscovering myself

In bars and cafes
In bylanes and alleys
In places that have all been home
In the knots I have tied
That over time
Weave into a beautiful crochet
That keeps me warm,
With memories and experiences
That make me, me

By Sarit

Youth

The dimples on my thighs
go by a different name called cellulite,
and no one finds them cute.

And the indelible crease on my right cheek,
that I thought I inherited from Papa is like
the yellow light, blinking at the crossroads of youth,
imminent of the approach of my 40s.

The Signs are all there,
everyone around me is getting Botox.

A prick in the forehead, to iron-out
the evidence of earned wisdom, experiences
now manifested as my frown deepens.

Dark brown-spots from the sunscreen-free playtime,
of our middle-class upbringing. And crows' feet
acquired through endless squinting to see the future more clearly.

Some are determined to erase the damage,
we inflicted on our bodies, in years of our invincible youth.

But the renewal I'd pay anything to have, would be
shots to temper pragmatism, the over-analysis of middle-age.

I'd happily be pricked to smoothen out wrinkles of self-doubt.
Or go under the knife to uncover the brazen person of my youth -
unburdened, untarnished in the absence of experience.

Because really that is what keeps me up at night,
not the cellulite, the imminent wrinkles or the crows-feet,
but the free-fall into conformity, and an unloved life.

By Neetika

House #3 Nirala Nagar

Stretched to its seams to contain
the ambitions of nine cousins on
their summer vacation, Nani's house was
the only witness of our afternoon play,
as our mothers napped post dal-bhaat lunches.

The garden became an ally as we trapped
bugs for our barbaric experiments.
And the undersides of beds our hiding spot,
until we were found and beaten by the oldest cousin.

Fueling our imaginations, the cotton curtains
danced at dusk, against the rare summer breeze.
As we gathered each day around Nani,
for an encore of our favorite ghost stories.

My memories of the sweltering summers
are still perfumed by the smell of the moist husks
of air cooler in the living room,
The sound of Doordarshan news coming on,
and the taste of Rooh Afza milk served at noon.

Evenings gave way to hopscotch in the front verandah,
until we heard the vroom from Mama's motorcycle.
Which always meant visits to the park and amusement rides,
or at the very least the promise of ice-cream.

I recall how swiftly black ants crawled on our skin as
we struggled to bring mangos down from the garden's singular tree.
And the 10 stitches to my palm, in the endeavor to sneakily make
sandwiches our for afternoon tea.

I remember how meticulously shares of Maggi were measured,
or the juiciness of Dasheri mangoes compared.
How the pistachio green wall of Nanaji's bedroom,
grew dirtier each year from our handprints and scuffles.

The days crawled,
but the summers dissolved swiftly.
When I look back now, it's hard to recall
if the house shrank overnight or gradually.

When the Siblings argued behind doors, we shrugged
Like us, their altercations were too without gravity?
Our young minds oblivious to
the unraveling knits of our family.

But as Nanaji withered away on a hospital bed
years later, the house became a battleground
and the prize to be won. Decaying walls, chipped paint,
and semi-kempt grass - valuable trophies.

While in our collective memories,
Nani's ghost stories, our whispered secrets at siesta,
and evening play lost their currency.

I have never been back, after its fate settled.
But I wonder if the other seven,
still look fondly back at those summers
at House #3 Nirala Nagar,
now preserved only in our memories.

By Neetika

Hum Dono Ki Yaadein

Mujhe tumhari Dadi ka ghar
bakhoobi yaad hai,
kuch is tarah jaise
hum dono ka bachpan
Lucknow mai guzra ho.

Woh verandah,
woh aangan,
woh aam ka pedh.

Mai aaj bhi tumharein
kisse kahaniyon mai,
keri ki khataas aur
ganj ki chaat dhoondta hun.

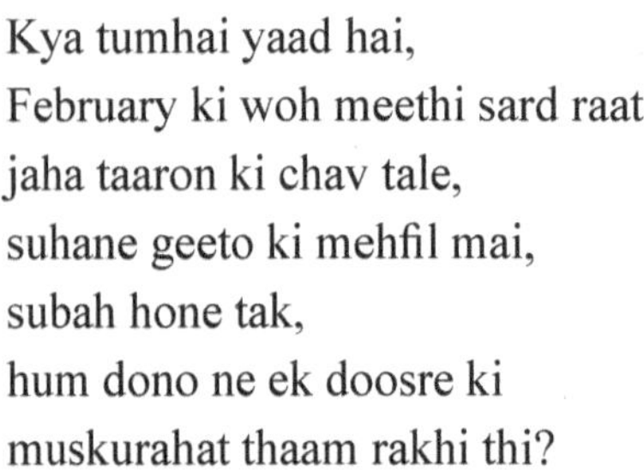

Kya tumhai yaad hai,
February ki woh meethi sard raat
jaha taaron ki chav tale,
suhane geeto ki mehfil mai,
subah hone tak,
hum dono ne ek doosre ki
muskurahat thaam rakhi thi?

Mai aaj bhi us raat ka
sureelapan dhoondta hun.
Woh geet yaad hai tumhai jo
videsh mai bethi, trunkcall ke zariye,
tum mere liye gun gunaya karti thi?

Abhi nahi aana sajna
Aaj jaane ki zidd na karo

Shayad woh aane jaane ki geet
humne itne gun gunaye, ke aaj bhi
zindagi mai therav dhoondte hai.

Hyderabad ka woh ghar toh
yaad hoga tumhai, jaha hum ek hi
shaam ke ganit mai, na jaane
kitne varsh ji gaye.
Us ghar ki rasoyi mai,
tumne mere haath ki
pehli chai pi thi, tabse ab tak,
tumhari subah ki chai, meri
sabse haseen zimmedari ban gayi.

Ek baat batao, aaj kal,
aadhi khuli, aadhi band
aankhon se, subah rasoi mai
chai ki patti dhoondti ho kya?

Kuch aesi hi hai, dhool mai lipti,
zehen mai bikhri, hothon par ruki,
panno par dodhti, hum dono ki yaadein

By Sarit

Ghar

Mera kal aur mera aaj
aksar aapas mai jhagadte rehte hai.
Aaj is baat se naraaz hai ki
pichle 9 saal mai 7 shahar badle hai mene.

Kal is baat se pareshaan ki har woh
bichda shahar mujhe ghar ki yaad dilata hai.
Har bichde ghar mai kuch na kuch bhool aaya hun.
Har naye ghar mai kuch na kuch gum ho jata hai.

Kabhi maa ka diya lihaaf, toh kabhi
baba ki di dua lakh dhoonde bhi nahi milti.

Kabhi kabhi behas mai,
aane wala kal bhi kood padhta hai.
Poochta hai, theraav ke baarein
mai kya khayal hai?

Kabhi tham kar, dheeme chalti hawa ko chehere par
mehsoos karne ke baarein mai kya socha hai?

Kabhi socha hai badalte shahar,
badalte mohalle, badalti galiyan,
badalte badalte kitna badal gaya mai?

Chalte chalte itna door nikal aaya mai ke
peeche mudh ke dekhu toh sab dhundla dikhta hai.
Raat ke andhere mai chupte chupate
jin galiyon ki jasoosi mai karta hun,
shayad bhool chuki hai woh galiyan mujhe.

Ya shayad aaj bhi intezaar hai unhe mera -
kayi shikayatein karni baki hai mujhse.
Bas milna nahi ho pata,
mere beetein hue kal ka, mere aaj se

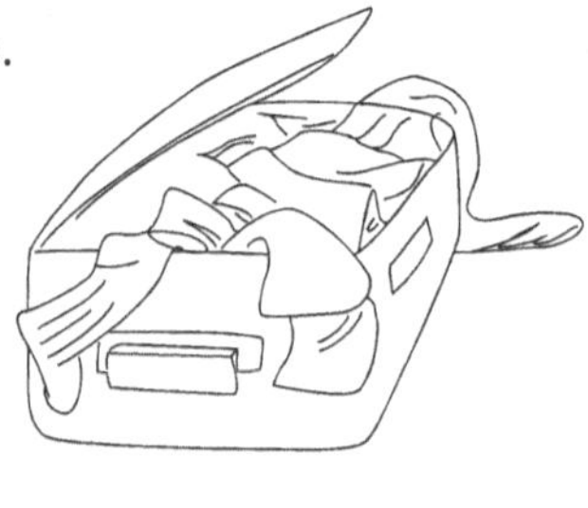

By Sarit

Safar

Mere mohalle ki tang galliyan kabhi
national highway dikha karti thi.
Kuch mera kad chotta tha, kuch
in galliyon ka dil bada

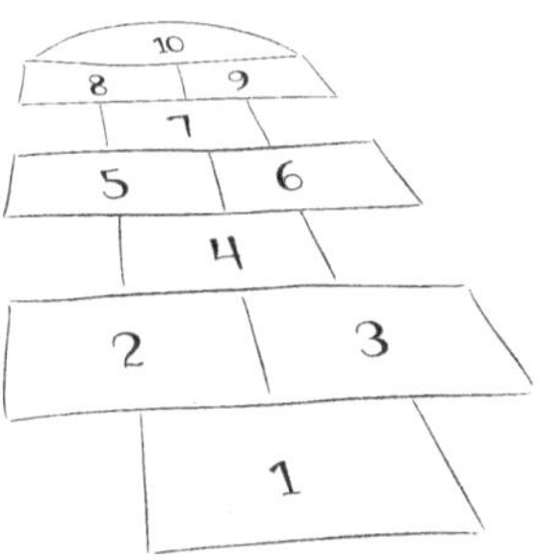

In galliyon mai hum
Pitthu ka Pyramid banate the.
Dhapa Aais Paais kehte shaam bitate the
Kabhi Action ke jutte pehen
diwar par chadh jaate the
Aur kabhi sabun ke bulbulo wali bandook
liye gundo se bhidh jaate the

Gali ke har doosre ladke ko
kaku bulate the
Aur jab maa ka diya ek rupaye ka sikka
ret mai gum ho jaata tha toh bokhla se jaate the

Aaj kal dukandaar se sikka nahi leta
Batue mai pada pichwade mai chubhta hai
Kaku bhi ab chupan chupayi nahi khelta
Bas mujh se chupta firta hai

Woh galiya woh bachpan zaroor mujhe farebi samajhte honge
Kehte honge ki bhale hi in tang galliyon mai
suraj ki taap nahi pahuch paati thi
Par chav toh humesha Rehti thi

Mera ghar jiske verrande mai ghutne chil Gaye the,
jiski chat par charpayi bichate the
Zaroor sochta hoga ki in 30 manzila imarato mai,
veranda kidhar hota hai?
Aur chat? Chat kiske hisse aati hai?

Ab kab tak baraamado, chato ka hisab lagayenge?
Har din tang hoti galliyon ki chaudayi, kab tak maap payenge?
Baat toh safar ki hai na, hai ke nahi?
Shiv nagar se gurgaon ka safar
Chicago se Toronto ka safar
Bachpan se jawani ka safar

By Sarit

Clutter

Many strangers occupy space in my room.
residing in nooks and crannies
I have overlooked for years.
Objects once adored, now foreign to me.

There are half-squeezed tubes of ointments,
for scars that have long since healed.
Memorabilia from people that are now just a blur -
neighbors in a nightstand drawer.

Talismans and chains, beads from broken jewelry,
that have been waiting for my time and attention.
Books weighed down by dust and negligence,
no longer stare back in anticipation.

Kafka's cracked silhouette
on a ceramic coaster, brought
from a back alley in Prague.
Clanking bronze, silver and gold medals -
artifacts from a bygone school history.

Unresolved tussles of charging cables,
concert tickets and a boarding pass -
evidence of summer's fables.
Miniature idols of Gods, a chair
that seats no one, a receptacle
for discarded clothes from each weary day.

I wonder how many of these objects I really loved,
How many did I really need?
How much of what I own is truly mine?
And how much will I get to keep?

By Neetika

Then and Now

How will we tell our children about the time
the world was forced to a screeching halt.
You and I, interrupted from our clamoring worldly hustle,
to be met by the silence of our home.

Slowed down to notice the way sunlight
played in different rooms at midday.
How it snuck into corners we forgot to dust;
altered the textures of surfaces where we lay.

A time to unearth buried talents -
your alchemy with cocktails, my experiments
with new recipes. Our collective wins and fails.

When fiction was inhaled and news was avoided.
When we finally became plant parents and
pondered about death and growing old.

And when the world slowly started turning again
I left the windows open to air out the fumes
of intimacy, that have seeped through
the crevices of our space. For two years, we were
forced indoors to find a home within our house.

I knew we would be fine, returning to our
old normal. But I worried for the couch,
the bed, and the desk - our allies
Would they miss the warmth of our company?

Would the ten plants we brought home,
yearn for our chatter over morning chai?

Who would now play audience to the
out-of-tune orchestra of our dishwasher
and the washing machine, or the whistling
of the perennially brewing caffeine?

How will we articulate, the dichotomy
of emotions we felt, as our days drifted
aimlessly into nights. Suspended between
fear and hope, our musings, reflections and fights.

I left the windows open to air out
the quiet realizations that began to surface within.
Perhaps a less structured life could be richer?
We didn't need to live less to have more,
Or wait for the weekend to look out the window.

By Neetika

The Serial Entrepreneur

Wake up one day,
no idea what hour of the day.
Slip on your denims, lace up your shoes,
and walk out into a world that doesn't give two hoots.

Your pupils shrink, it's far too bright.
Before you know it, it's way past midnight.
While everyone else sees a deep indigo night,
you see never-ending light

You hop on your bike, rally your friends.
Set out on a journey, you hope never ends.
You ride together, humming a song
no one else will ever sing.

Auditions follow, polite applause soon after.
Others join in and the noise gets louder.
The ride gets tough, the terrain harder,
but you stay on and persevere.

As the fight gets tougher, the struggle more real,
you look back at the ones who dropped out.
Some screaming – I told you so.
You look at the ones who have come this far,
still preparing for the next round.

The song still ringing through your ears,
you struggle to hide your fears
Barely managing to hold back tears,
still, you peel back the layers,

You find whatever is left of you, left within you.
With anxiety and gratitude,
you slip on your denims,
lace up your shoes.
You walk back out in a world
that does not give two hoots.

By Sarit

22 yards

Have you ever watched middle aged men
defy themselves and stretch beyond anatomy?
All to chase a red cherry?

Have you ever watched a boy
with that same red cherry in his hand,
stride towards another with a willow in hand?

It is the most beautiful thing in the world,
spread across 22 yards and 22 souls - each
looking to relive an entire childhood In a single afternoon.

When I feel lost, I return to the place I grew up.
A place I could no longer grow in.
Only to find myself in a place I no longer recognised,

I was searching for myself but what I found
was a cricket ground, a willow, a cherry, 22 yards
and a team - where I was just one part of a whole.

I have learnt a way of life between those 22 yards -
a life that is selfless; built in partnerships.

I can close my eyes and remember every single time
a ball has hit the middle of my bat. Every single time
the hair on the back of my neck stood up in applause.

Words of wisdom from my batting partner
Ringing in my ears - "Relax, calm down, you got this!"

It is on that turf of green, under a blue sky,
between 22 yards, chasing a red cherry -
that's where I find my most authentic self

Loud, aggressive, fearless, me!
A happy me!

By Sarit

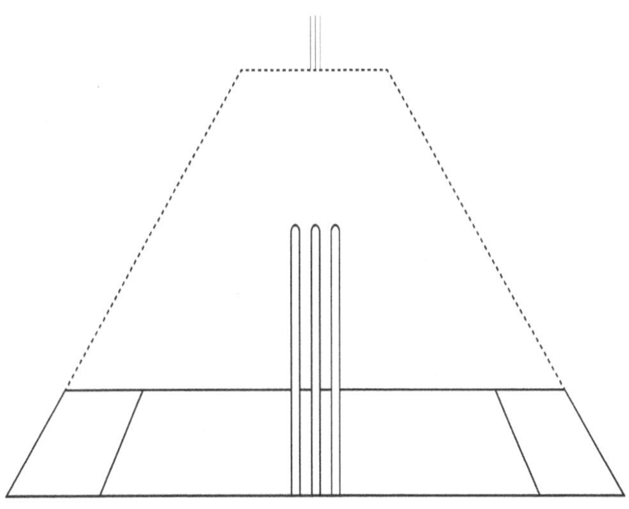

Behen

Bachpan ke khelo mein
mai kabhi cheating nahi kar pata tha
Dost behen ki kasam dila dete the
aur main jhooth nahi bol pata tha

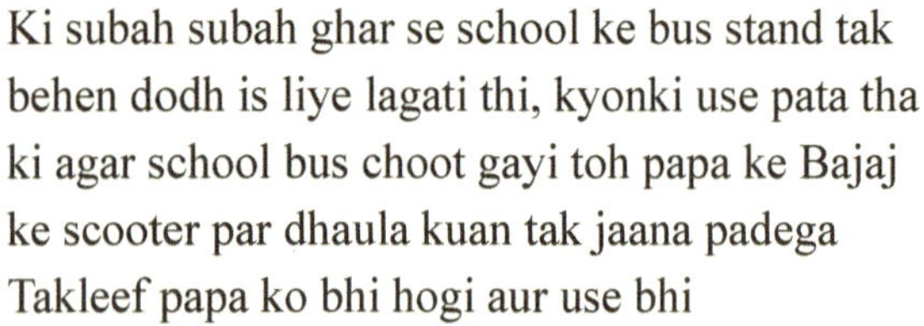

Bahut pyara rishta tha behen ka aur mera
Mujhse sirf do saal badi thi, par
mujhse bahut pehle badi ho gayi thi

Shayad ghar ke haalat
jinhai mai umar bhar nakaarta raha,
usne umar se pehle samajh liye the

Ki subah subah ghar se school ke bus stand tak
behen dodh is liye lagati thi, kyonki use pata tha
ki agar school bus choot gayi toh papa ke Bajaj
ke scooter par dhaula kuan tak jaana padega
Takleef papa ko bhi hogi aur use bhi

Bahut ladte the hum bachpan mein
Behen kabhi mujhe chatt par band kar deti thi,
toh kabhi store room mein

Apni ice cream poori khatam karke, meri khane
aa jaati thi. Mai tilmilata rahta tha, aur woh hasti khelti

Kisi nayi shararat mai lag jaati -
school ki bus ke peeche dodhte dodhte,
ek din usne Australia ki flight pakdi,
aur mujhse bahut door ho gayi

Chutiyon mai milne aati thi kabhi kabhi
Un mehmano ki tarah, jo tohfe toh laate hai,
par saath hi aapka kamra bhi hathya lete hai

Uska Australia jaana, humarein beech aaye faansle
ki shuruat thi. Fir naukri, shadi, bache -
Zindagi ke har padhav ke saath, meri behen
se judi har umeed dheere dheere khatam hoti gayi

Kuch 15 saal pehle Melbourne ke chote se ghar mein,
gale lag kar khoob roye the hum dono
Ek arse baad khulke ek doosre se shikayat kari thi

Kabhi kabhi man karta hai woh shaam
wapas laut aaye, jaha mai aur meri didi,
ek doosre se woh saari shikayatein kar paye
jo hum waqt rehte nahi kar paye

Shayad samajh paye hum ek doosre ko
Humarei beech ke faansle ko
Aur har us beete lamhe ko
Jaha hum dono behtar ho sakte the

Ek doosre se sehmat ho sakte the
Ek doosre ke saath khade ho sakte the
Ek doosre ke liye zindagi behtar kar sakte the

Shayad beete lamho ke gile shikwe,
aane wale barso ka marham ban sake

By Sarit

For Dad

I am only just beginning to understand
the struggles of making a marriage work.
From expectations, to the disappointment of not meeting them.
From constant quarrels and arguments to the
shared cup of morning tea enjoyed on our verandah

I am only just beginning to recognise
the effort of bringing up two kids -
Driving them to school on a two wheeler
they were too embarrassed to ride.
Breaking the bank for their tuition and
struggling to put food on their plate.
From them growing into adults, to them
growing too old for your humble home.

I am only just beginning to comprehend
your helplessness at watching your parents age.
Like I watch you now from a distance.
Your tired legs can't carry your weight anymore.
You've lost most of your teeth to diabetes
Yet every morning before you put on your dentures,
you send me a good morning message.

A video call is too much - to look at you
through the phone screen, your body frail,
your face old, with a toothless smile.

I am overwhelmed with feelings
of wanting to be like you.
Hoping I don't end up like you.
Wishing you had a better life.

By Sarit

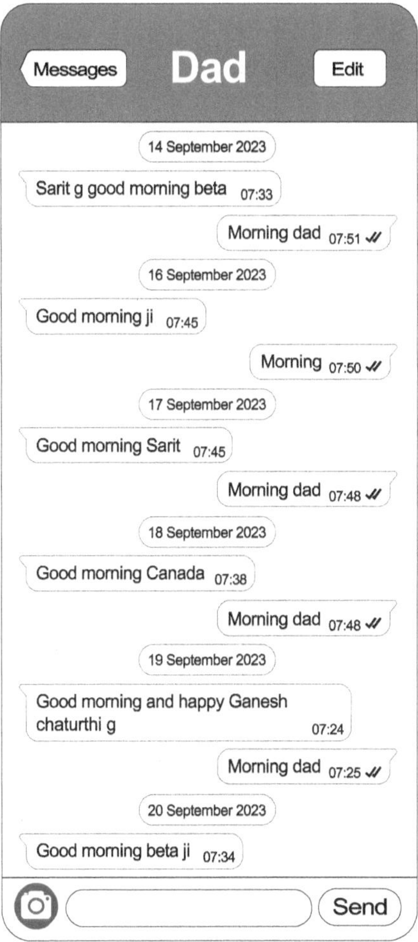
Messages
Dad
Edit
14 September 2023
Sarit g good morning beta 07:33
Morning dad 07:51
16 September 2023
Good morning ji 07:45
Morning 07:50
17 September 2023
Good morning Sarit 07:45
Morning dad 07:48
18 September 2023
Good morning Canada 07:38
Morning dad 07:48
19 September 2023
Good morning and happy Ganesh chaturthi g 07:24
Morning dad 07:25
20 September 2023
Good morning beta ji 07:34
Send

Maa

Maa ko kisi jyotish ne bataya tha -
pani se khatra hai bete ko

Maa ne jyotish ki baat kuch aise
gaanth baandh li jaise abhi koi lehar
aayegi aur baha ke le jayegi mujhko.

Mere doobne ka itna dar tha maa ko
ki kabhi terna nahi seekhaya -
shikayat nahi, baat kar raha hun.

Bachpan ke kisso mai,
maa ko yaad kar raha hun.

Ek baar maa se jhagad kar Rishikesh
ghoomne nikal gaya. Maa bahut naraaz thi.

Meri rafting karne ki zidd, ladakpan ka
aakrosh, aur jyotish ki baat -
kuch theek nahi lag raha tha maa ko.

Aur mai?
Mai bekhauf, rubber ki nav mai
hawa bhar, Ganga mai kood gaya!
Agle 60 minute tak bas ek naraaz nadi,
nadi ki gusel lehron ka shor aur
un lehron se jhagadta mai.

Yaad nahi kab pani ka bahav
shaant hua, bas itna yaad hai,
tab shaam ki aarti ka samay ho raha tha.

Door kahi mandir mai ghanti baj rahi thi
aur suraj kinare ke pare
raat ke andhere mai khone ko tha.

Sab tham sa gaya tha,
sab gum sa ho gaya tha.

Bas ek ahsas baki tha jaise ek bahut
bura samay tal gaya ho. Mano jaise
chot lagne ke baad maa ne god mai bhar liya ho.

Dheere dheere pani se bhi dosti ho gayi -
uske baad pani se shayad kabhi dar laga hi nahi.

Aaj kal ek badi jheel ke paas rehta hun,
sukoon ke paas ekant ke kinaare.

Maa ki har kahi baat, har bewajah
ka veham, aur maa ki har dua ne,
aaj bhi sambhal rakha hai mujhe.

By Sarit

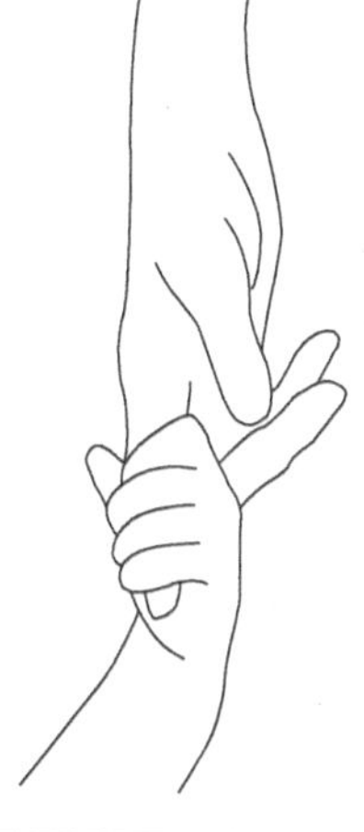

Inheritance

Tucked behind my grandfather's diaries,
a black-and-white photo of a girl in her teens -
my mum unrecognizable in a well-oiled bob;
the brownest eyes I have ever seen.

In a old family album, I find a picture of dad -
mustached, half his current age and size,
bathed in a European glow, deep in thought.

These are not the version of my parents I know,
but somehow, these versions live in me.

Dad's Lucknowi biryani recipe, that
I learnt, then tweaked, to suit my
worldly palate. Mama's old Banarasis,
cut up for the yearly festivities.

The shrillness of my mother's voice,
finds a new identity in me.
Dad's no-nonsense façade and temperament,
have often been used as adjectives to describe me.

Our collective love for paan, our disdain
for hypocrisy. My father's views on politics,
that shaped my liberal rebellion. Mom's
hoarding tendencies fuelling the minimalist in me.

It hits me, the void they speak of -
If I remain childless, there will be
no one to unearth or relive my youth.
No one to inherit my love for yoga,
or loathe my need for discipline.

Who would piece together the
puzzle of my life from stacks of
unfinished poems and junk jewellery?

Children are perhaps a tool for immortality -
keeper of our dreams, carriers of our memories.
So when my parents say ever-so-often,
"You'll know when you have children"
It is perhaps to convey the solace they find
in the knowledge that somehow their story,
will find its epilogue through me.

By Neetika

Waiting

I sat across,
as the doctor laid out the plan.

I was only half-listening.
Knowing that none of this would matter.
In a few months we would be parents!

The doctor's lips moved, but
my mind was elsewhere.
Reliving the steps that got us here.

We hadn't been trying for very long
But it felt like it had been a while.

Just getting to the doctor's desk
was a journey, a mechanical process.

Tracking ovulation on fertility apps,
fighting anxiety, stress and fatigue to
make the most of a ten day window.

A window I feared everytime it came knocking
What if I can't, what if I can?
What comes after that?

What came after was the neverending waiting
that ended with a small white stick and the letters
Y E S

I sat across the doctor thinking
about the night that got us here -
the warmth and intimacy that broke through
all the mechanics that came before it.
It had to be that night!

Soon after that day at the clinic, I left.
We were moving to a new country,
and I was house hunting

Every house I saw, I asked myself -
Could I see the three of us living here?
Would we be able to walk down with a stroller
and walk right into the greens?

I finalized a unit that had childcare
on the ground floor and a beautiful
maternity boutique steps from our apartment building.

It was all going as per plan, until
the readings plateaued. The scans blurred.
We went from sharing the size of the foetus,
to the termination of a potentially dangerous pregnancy.

A month later, you came home alone
I adopted the - It's ok, it will be fine, role.
Even though it wasn't ok, it wasn't fair,
I wasn't fine.

It is particularly hard every day
when I walk past that boutique
It's hard when on our ride down the elevator,
a little girl in her stroller grabs your finger
and refuses to let go.

We often joke about children we
are close to, kids we've seen grow up -
we tell each other, let's go steal one.
We joke about how some parents have one too many.

Behind the banter sits a prickly pain that
refuses to go away. So we are back
to the mechanics. The process that often
leads to intimacy and waiting and hope.

Most of all hope.

By Sarit

Julie

It was late 2009 when I first met her,
with a bag of Pedigree and some flowers.

Julie and I hit it off instantly. Our first
meeting and every one thereafter like
a well-choreographed song and dance sequence.

Her howling from her room as I was climbing
the stairs, nearing the door. I could hear her paws
sliding and gliding across the room, making
a screeching noise against the marble floor.

By the time I rang the doorbell, she was
already leaning against the door. As soon as I
got in, she would catapult herself onto me -
her paws off the floor, And me on all fours!

Every time we met, all through our courtship,
I had a great relationship with all of Neetika's family.
And when we drifted apart, I found many whys.
The only thing I never found a why for was
betraying Julie's unconditional love.

It was 2013 when Neetika and I got married.
When Julie and I met after the wedding,
it was the same song and dance routine.
She didn't complain about the lost time.

She was just happy I was back -
with a bag of Pedigree and flowers.

It must have been the bag of Pedigree that
won her over. Julie and I were both hardcore foodies.
She always wanted a part of every meal.
If you know me you'd know, Sarit doesn't share food.

But Julie never took no for an answer -
our meals had a familiar sight too, her paws on my lap,
some chicken curry on my plate and some licked
clean off the floor. She always ate with us.
And she always ate from our plates.

Another thing we had in common was our vanity.
Julie was too proud to mingle with other doggos, she
would also hide in a corner after every summer cut that
parted her from her magnificent fur.

In 2020 during the pandemic, we spent
a lot of time together. She still wanted the
chicken curry, but couldn't digest it anymore.
She would lick the floor clean, only for us
to wipe it clean soon after.

She couldn't jump on the bed anymore.
It was difficult for her to carry her weight.
I would help her climb up on the bed where
she would snuggle between Neetika and me.

She started hating us leaving the house
Everytime we got ready to head out
A slow walk to the door, and parking
herself there till we returned became
her favorite forms of protest.

It was 2022, when I got a message from Dad.
None of us had the courage to tell Neetika.
None of us did. I remember I cried for less than a minute,
I had to jump on a work call that took priority over my grief.

And just like that, Julie's loss got buried under
meeting minutes, house moves, and visa applications.
I have cried a number of times since,
remembering Julie, trying to forget Julie.

It was 2023, at the drive test center - the lady
across the counter was telling me about her aging father,
and in the midst of our conversation she said,
"Not everyone is fortunate enough to grow old"

Julie was, she grew old.
Like a lady - calm, poised and elegant.
Like a granny, clad in a cotton saree
with a zari border. Giving and receiving love -
to and from everyone around her.

In Julie I saw a full circle of life.
A glorious life

By Sarit

When Words Collide

Your voice found me first,
at the back of the classroom where I sat bored.
Before I could trace it, your tall, lanky frame
commanded nearly a hundred heads.
How could an 18-year-old be so self-assured?

I was the new girl no one noticed,
you had a girlfriend. I overheard you
brag at the college canteen. I must
have rolled my eyes and thought how lame.

Then one afternoon you ambled over,
to sit with us for lunch. No longer
in awe of that popular guy from a distance.
The spell was broken, I guess we could be friends.

Through hours spent outside the
print shop beneath that facade,
I glimpsed a loner. Maybe you and I
both didn't fit in; but you definitely tried harder.

So it wasn't completely absurd that
friends became lovers. Back then,
love was the lyrics to Coldplay's 'Yellow',
and the artless romance of 'Before Sunrise'.

We both knew heartbreak, yes.
But partnership?
How bold (or fatal?) to dive right in
without trying it on for size.

Blame our age, or blame patriarchy -
we unraveled, so we could walk
our separate inward journeys.

And if truth be told, the luster of our story,
of how we finally married each other, has worn on me.
But between our ludo and screaming matches,
your oscillating obsession with food and cricket,
your complex relationship with money,
in your nuances and annoyances,
my partner - it was in the mundane of our marriage,
that I truly found you.

By Neetika

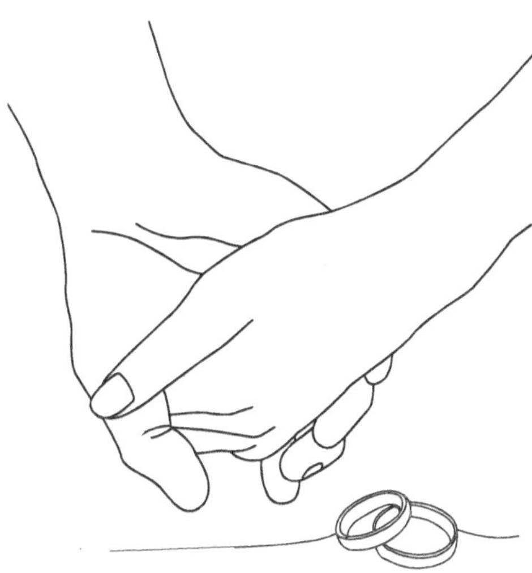

Summer Scene

Your head
tranquil
on my thigh.

The canopy
of leaves above
transforming sunlight
into dots around our bodies.

I stop
the ants
from invading
our 2x2 mats.

You play
with
my belly button.

I read
punctuated only by
the frenzy of birds,
and the occasional honk
of Friday traffic.

Your story
hangs
mid-sentence.

As you watch
dogs ambling
towards their owners.

Sometimes
I lightly touch your hand
to point out,
a blissfully-asleep
occupant
in a stroller.

We witness
silhouettes
failing at Hula Hoop
and
paper boats launched
in park puddles.

I smell
tacos
from picnic tables,
and pray
for 7pm
coffee-drinkers
On the benches.

Conversations
and crickets
compete
to swallow
the silence of
this summer scene.

We take turns
to devour
tart raspberry ice-cream.

I wonder
if it is possible
to be unhappy
on a
good
summer day.

By Neetika

Acknowledgements

Thank you to Young Orators Club Secundrabad for being my safe space

Thank you to Atta Galata and Let Poetry be for being my outlet in Bangalore

Thank you to Team Invictus for always being my best eleven

Thank you to BuildSupply for all the lessons

Thank you to friends and family who offered advise generously

Thank you to everyone whose kept reading all this while

Thank you to Mohammed Ahmed Saadeldin A. for capturing the essence of our words in his illustrations and the cover page.

Thank you to Rochelle D'Silva for all the poetry workshops, feedback, for being our editor and most of all for being a friend.

Dedications

To our language teachers

Neetika - Late Mam Sadhna Vyas who encouraged me to never stop writing.

Sarit - Kanta Dhingra Mam for seeing beyond the boy who stammered.

To Julie who is in our hearts forever.

About authors

Neetika went to school for architecture and urban planning. She now works as an interior designer in North America and enjoys telling stories through her words and designs. Her quest for a forever home has her currently stradelling between three cities New Delhi, Chicago and Toronto.

Caught between technology and the built environment Sarit graduated as a building architect and currently practices product management. Having lived in 8 cities across three countries over the last decade Sarit is most proud of his learnings as a co-founder, a cricketer and a wanderer.

www.ingramcontent.com/pod-product-compliance
Lightning Source LLC
LaVergne TN
LVHW040920150826
845672LV00007B/2127

9798891861862